# Seminex 2.0

## *The Foundational Heresy* that Has Propelled the LCMS from Explosion to Implosion

This essay first appeared in Christian News,
Volume 63, No. 12, March 24, 2025

Rev. Gregory P. Schulz, D.Min., Ph.D.
*The Lutheran School of Theology, Kenya*

https://lutheranphilosopher.com

ISBN #979-8-9895813-4-4

# Seminex 2.0

## *The Foundational Heresy* that Has Propelled the LCMS from Explosion to Implosion

### Rev. Gregory P. Schulz, D.Min., Ph.D.
*The Lutheran School of Theology, Kenya*

As we enter Lent 2025 it is safe to say that the 2024 observances of the so-called Fiftieth Anniversary of the Seminex Walkout from our St. Louis seminary are done. The symposiums and conferences, the publishing, postings, and social media comments have all run their course. Seminex is in the books. However, the heresy of Seminex is not over and done with in the Lutheran Church-Missouri Synod. Far from it.

The theological and historical analyses of Seminex have failed to bring into the light of day the metaphysical or *foundational heresy* that made Seminex possible. Kurt Marquart, of blessed memory, alluded to this underlying heresy when he wrote this in the years right after the St. Louis controversy in the 1970s:

> It is important to see that the uncompromising supremacy of 'scientific' reasoning in the ... critical method is not an excess or an abuse which can somehow be tempered. On the contrary, it is of the essence of the method. Science has no room for privileged authority or sacrosanct texts (*Anatomy of an Explosion*, hereafter written *Explosion*).

There are two crucial terms for us to keep in mind,

namely, *scientific method* and *authoritative or sacrosanct texts*. I will provide an overview of the modern scientific method under the upcoming heading Modernism and Seminex 1.0. The privileged authority and sacrosanct texts in this citation from Marquart's *Explosion* refers in the first place to Christ's divine authority expressed in the Holy Scriptures and also to the authoritative Lutheran Confessions which partake of our Lord's divine authority because, as the Formula of Concord puts it, the written Word of Christ is the foundation, rule, and norm by which all dogmas ought to be judged and by which all controversies that arise must be explained and decided in a Christian way. The foundational heresy targets Christ's divine authority expressed in the Scriptures and the Lutheran Confessions by confusing and misleading those who read or interpret the Scriptures. It also effects those who may want to read the Bible.

To uncover the foundational heresy that made Seminex possible, we must first agree on what the terms *philosophy, heresy, hermeneutics,* and *language* mean. Because the divine gift of language is widely misunderstood, I will give special attention to defining and reiterating what language is in a careful phenomenological manner. The reason that we badly misunderstand what language is, and therefore feel free to weaponize and abuse language as if it were our own invention, tool, or plaything, is the widespread acceptance today of the foundational heresy which is the topic of this essay.

It will help to trace out, very briefly, the anti-intellectual, anti-Christ philosophy of language that lies behind modern science (as Marquart mentions in *Explosion*), and then becomes manifest in postmodernism (as I explain briefly but with philosophical care in my *Anatomy of an Implosion,* hereafter written *Implosion*). I will follow my sketch of postmodernism's philosophy of language, the anti-Logos, anti-authority philosophy of language which I am calling *the foundational heresy,* with the evidence that Seminex is not over and done with. On the contrary, the Missouri Synod over the past twenty years or so has become Seminex 2.0.

## The *foundational heresy* of Seminex 1.0

When I say that the Seminex heresy at its core is a metaphysical or foundational heresy, I have in mind Colossians 2:8-9. Let me translate the first of these two verses from the Saint Paul's Greek this way: "Be on guard that no one takes you captive through a hollow and inherently deceptive philosophy, the kind that is grounded in merely human hand-me-downs and the ABCs of the secular world—but *not grounded in Christ.*" Philosophy that is not *kata Christon* (Paul's Greek) is necessarily hollow and deceptive because it is not based on Christ and His Word. As the apostle explains in 1 Corinthians 1, a chapter that is a doctrinal center of gravity for our Lutheran theology of the cross, Paul identifies Christ as the *sophos* or wisdom of God incarnate. The Greek philosophers earnestly wanted to befriend wisdom (*philo-sophos*), and Paul had substantial face-to-face time with Him (see 1 Corinthians 1:18ff and Proverbs 8:22ff; Acts 22:17-21).

When talking about heresy, we know that its Latin root is *hæresis*, from which we learn that a heresy is a school of philosophical thought—where *philosophy* means "all intellectual or academic work (an umbrella term covering all the academic disciplines that we can name today). Augustine uses *philosophandi* in *City of God*, Book 19, for example, for all serious study and learning. I am especially concerned, though, with the Greek use of *hairesis* as a verb in the middle voice, where the user of the heresy, we are taught by the middle voice, is simultaneously (a) promulgating the heresy and (b) working under its influence, whether consciously or unconsciously.

The heresy of Seminex is usually identified as a hermeneutical *heresy;* that is, a Bible interpretation heresy. But I am arguing that St. Louis's hermeneutic heresy was made possible by a deeper, metaphysical heresy aimed at our trust in the foundation, the Rock of our salvation, Christ Himself—a heresy designed to make us all incredulous of any authoritative written texts, including especially the Bible—and to make us believe that language, especially written language, is inherently meaningless and open to any and all interpretations. The Church's one Foundation, Jesus Christ the Rock, is impervious to heresy, but the members of His Church are vulnerable to heresy, as the New Testament epistles make crystal clear. So, I am not speaking about a heresy that exists somehow in the foundation, a *foundation* heresy. My concern is with a powerful heresy targeting people, a heresy capable of miseducating people to such an extent that they despair of the meaningfulness of language and willfully interpret even authoritative, normative texts according to their own changing needs and desires. This is why it is a *foundational* heresy.

The foundational heresy undergirding the Seminex walkout over fifty years ago works in such a way that it transfers all interpretive authority or hermeneutics to the professor (or reader), and seduces him into doing whatever he wants with authoritative texts, whether the text is the American Declaration of Independence, The Formula of Concord, or the Word of God. From the lesser to the greater, these are examples of the sacrosanct texts Marquart was writing about.

What I am arguing is that the Seminex heresy was

not (and is not) just another instance of false doctrine. It was and is no ordinary explosion; rather, Seminex was the test firing of a weapon of mass destruction that hit St. Louis in the 1970s. Seminex was the prototype of a weapon of mass destruction (WMD) that targets the very medium in which we read, mark, and inwardly digest God's Word. As I teach regarding the philosophy of language, language is what we would call philosophically a *given*, and which is, in reality, a *divine gift*. The foundational heresy aims to make us incredulous or disbelieving of this divine gift of language altogether.

To paraphrase Paul in Acts 17, "In language (language as *LOGOS*, see John 1) we live and move and have our being." The atmosphere in which we live and exist as human beings is language. The inerrant and efficacious language of Scripture (Isaiah 55), and our everyday fallible but inherently meaningful language are on the same spectrum; they are the same phenomenon, the same divine gift. The essential difference between our everyday language and writing (this essay, for example) and the Bible is that the biblical text is unsurpassably authoritative, the most sacrosanct of all sacrosanct texts. In philosophical terms, the written text of the Word of God is *maximally normative*. That is the meaning of the term *norm* in the first part of our Formula of Concord, the Thorough Declaration, which is titled The Comprehensive Summary, Foundation, Rule, and Norm.

Furthermore, the foundational heresy turns out to be a heresy against humanity, since each one of us is made in the image of God and meant for fellowship with God and our neighbor—within the medium or the atmosphere of language. In *Politics*, Book 1 Aristotle shares his discovery that human beings are distinguished from all other beings *essentially*, as the language (Greek, *logos*) species. Further, Aristotle recognizes that language or *logos* makes human fellowship (*koinonia* in Aristotle's Greek) possible. As the pagan but gifted philosopher could not know, language also makes God's fellowship with us possible. Luther stipulates Aristotle's minimum philosophical definition of the human being in the opening propositions of his 1536 Disputation Concerning Man. Language, as the Psalm for Lent 1 teaches us in the reading and praying of the text, is what makes us unlike "a horse or mule without understanding, that must be controlled with bit and bridle..." (Psalm 32:9).

To reiterate, Seminex's hermeneutic was made possible by an anti-Christ and anti-Bible philosophy of language, a foundational heresy that was widely presupposed or taken for granted without talking about it. In the century before Seminex the heresy governing the hermeneutic innovations of Seminex would have been identified as *modernism*, but coming out of the closet at the same time that the Seminex professors and supporters were making their dramatized exit from the seminary, it was already becoming clear that modernism's displacement of authority from the sacrosanct text of the Bible was coming to its inevitable culmination in the denial of all meaning to all texts and language. This logical and deeply heretical outcome of modernism is what we know as *postmodernism*. Postmodernism's philosophy of language is the foundational heresy. Time to begin connecting the dots.

**Modernism and Seminex 1.0**

Our old evil foe did not take the German Reformation lying down. Barely fifty years after Martin Luther and the confessors of the German Reformation deconstructed the papacy (in German philosophy, *deconstructing* means to eliminate the crust and the rust, the distractions and the accretions around the text in order to read that written text as it is), Cartesian rationalism in the 1600s and then Humean scientific empiricism in the 1700s, created the prototype foundational heresy for Seminex in the 1970s. Recall Marquart's *anatomy*, or analysis of the scientific methodology of the Seminex heresy, and his insight that science has no room for privileged authority (such as that of our Lord Jesus, Mathew 28:18) or for sacrosanct texts, particularly the text of the Bible.

Satan's predicament after the Reformation was a *jeremiad* moment for him, so to speak. As we can read in Jeremiah 36, while Jehudi read from the first edition scroll of the book of Jeremiah, every three or four columns or so King Jehoiakim would slice the autograph words off the scroll of the Scriptures and incinerated the words of God in his blazing fire until the entire scroll was consumed, while his administrators stood by, oblivious and fearless. Because of that, the Lord put a stop to Jehoiakim and his entire family line. Then He had Jeremiah produce a second first edition of Jeremiah's biblical book. All this put an eternal stop to any and every effort to eliminate the biblical text. So, the only move left for our enemy after the Reformation was *to keep people away from* the biblical text—to teach them to doubt, distrust, disdain language, the singular medium or means of grace for access to the Lord's steadfast love and expressed will. Cutting off access to the means of grace is the project of modernism, right down to the European Enlightenment and beyond.

Renee Descartes initiated modernism and its downgrading of language at the very beginning of modernity in the 1600's, the start of the Scientific Revolution. As first-time readers of *Principles of Philosophy* can tell, while Descartes necessarily has to do his thinking in language, he urgently wants to convince his readers to doubt the trustworthiness of everything outside our own minds, including authoritative texts. He does this by relocating ideas and thoughts in the individual's mind from the public space of language into the privacy of the human mind. "I am a mental being. I think, therefore I exist." Descartes was a *rationalist,* meaning that he relied heavily on innate ideas—the idea of a triangle, for instance—already in the private mind (he imagined) to articulate an early version of what we know as the scientific method. See his *Discourses on the Method,* Part 6 for his commitment, in addition, to his modernist relocation of authority from written texts to scientific methodology.

David Hume, a scientific empiricist in the 1700s, furthered the notion that ideas are only in the mind, even though it remained obvious that thinking and reasoning take place in the medium of the *public domain* or *atmosphere* of language. As an empiricist who aspired to be the Isaac Newton of human nature, he insisted that bona fide ideas are ideas that come through the senses but are connected within and utilized by one's private, scientifically educated mind. At the end of his *An Enquiry Concerning Human Understanding,* you will find his dramatic way of discounting the authority of sacrosanct texts and theology (remember Marquart pointing out that science has no room for sacred texts) that we refer to as Hume's Fork. I call it "Hume's Pitch Fork."

> When we run over libraries, convinced of these principles [of empirical scientific fact], what havoc must we make? If we take in hand any volume of school metaphysics [that is, theology], for instance; let us ask, *Does it contain any abstract reasoning concerning quantity or number?* No. *Does it contain any experimental reasoning concerning matter of fact and existence?* No. Commit it then to the flames: For it can contain nothing but sophistry

and illusion.

Notice the replacement of authoritative texts on theology and metaphysical matters with the authority of metrics, math, and scientific facts.

As a relevant aside, at the end of his earthly life, before slipping into a coma and dying a few days later, Hume revised his *Dialogues Concerning Natural Religion* and concluded his philosophical oeuvre by writing that every educated person should be skeptical of modern philosophy and flee to the revealed truth of Scripture. Modern philosophers do not know what to make of this anomaly, which is another indication of the widespread dismissal of biblical authority, which is the hallmark of modernism.

> A person, seasoned with a just sense of the imperfections of natural reason, will fly to revealed truth with the greatest avidity: While the haughty dogmatist, persuaded that he can erect a complete system of theology by the mere help of philosophy, disdains any further aid and rejects this adventitious instructor. To be a philosophical skeptic is, in a man of letters, the first and most essential step towards being a sound, believing *Christian*.

After Hume came the 1800s, the century that provided the Seminex professors with their "historical critical" method of biblical interpretation. This was the century of Hegel, Darwin, Marx, and Nietzsche. It will be enough for our purposes to mention that the highly influential German thinker, GFW Hegel, an older contemporary of CFW Walther, a founding pastor of the LCMS, utterly dismissed Christ and His written Word from academia while, at the same time, ransacking biblical and theological vocabulary for words he could interpret and use however he chose. Having untethered philosophy from the biblical text and its divine authority, Hegel repurposed words such as Spirit, Will, and Freedom so that he could do "philosophy as mythology" (J. Glenn Gray). His famous *dialectical materialism* was a pattern and a method for self-enclosed dialogue and self-interpretation about the meaning and purpose of history from which Christ and the Bible (unless one would render Scripture mythologically) were methodically excluded.

In modernity, knowledge (the philosophical term is *epistemology*) starts and ends with human tradition and the ABCs of the secularizing world (remember Colossians 2:8). The nineteenth century marks the official Western rejection of the *Nisi Per Verbum* of our Apology, Article 4, from the sixteenth century: "God cannot be apprehended or dealt with except through the Word," which is Christ, the Bible, and necessarily, language or *logos*.

For matters of history and the meaning of life—well, this will naturally have to be addressed by means of meaningful myths, according to the modernists. A society after the fullness of time that rejects Christ and His Word can only ape the pagan societies before the fullness of time and interpret life mythologically. This is *modernism*. Modernism is the inkpot into which the Seminexers dipped their pens and their brains before teaching biblical hermeneutics. For a memorable, usable, honest analysis of the religious consequences of modernism, read Nietzsche's Parable of the Madman in *The Joyful Science,* written on the cusp of the 1900s, the century of Seminex.

So, the heretical hermeneutics of the Seminex professors, in which they played with the written text of Holy Scripture by means of a scientific methodology, were based on *modernism*—a methodology that put science and a scientific epistemology between the efficacious Word of God and the reader. It is worth noting at this point that the Seminex hermeneutics were as unacademic as they were un-Lutheran.

The oh-so academic Seminex professors who marched out of the St. Louis seminary were oh-so ignorant of the powerful case being made in the early and late 20$^{th}$ century against modernism's disdain of language. In the first half of the century, Ludwig Wittgenstein, a reader of the Lutheran existentialist thinker Søren Kierkegaard, dealt a body blow to modernism's dismissal of language with his *Tractatus Logico-Philosophicus.* Martin Heidegger, a dutiful reader of the Greek New Testament and of Luther's writings (Heidegger did not die until a couple of months after the Seminex walkout on February 19, 1974), had been unpacking his thesis, "Language is the house of [the human] being" in *On the Way to Language,* a series of essays that were translated into English in 1971. In *Truth and Method,* under the section in Part III headed Word and Verbum, Hans-Georg Gadamer had concluded, "The cornerstone of Christian thought [our Lord's incarnation] is all the more important for us because for Christian thought too the incarnation is closely connected to the problem of the word." The first English version was published in 1971; this major twentieth-century work had been available in German since 1960.

## Postmodernism and Seminex 2.0

The Seminex heretics and their supporters were operating under the influence of modernism, but modernism was being assimilated and improved by a philosophy (more properly, an anti-philosophy) known as *postmodernism*. In 1979, the decade of Seminex 1.0, Jean-François Lyotard published *Report on Knowledge,* which included this definition of postmodernism: "Simplifying to the extreme, I define postmodernism as incredulity towards metanarratives." This means, "Postmodernism is a philosophy of incessant doubt regarding any authoritative text." As you can read for yourself online at The Stanford Encyclopedia of Philosophy, "That postmodernism is indefinable is a truism." This is a clue about the demonic power of the foundational heresy of postmodernism. Postmodernism denies the inherent meaningfulness of language before, during, and after using language to convince us that language is meaningless. You can imagine what this methodical, philosophical incredulity or disbelief of authoritative texts does to postmodernists' own writing.

Not only was modernism and its scientific denial of textual authority all the rage at the Saint Louis seminary in the 1970s; it was also the case that the Seminex 1.0 decade was the debut decade of postmodernism in the United States, with the publication of Jacques Derrida's *Of Grammatology, Writing and Difference,* and *Margins of Philosophy*. Most people think of Derrida in connection with *deconstruction* (a bastardization of deconstruction in German philosophy), a force-multiplying feature of the foundational heresy. Derrida was in the process of sowing continual doubt about the meaningfulness of language as the linchpin to his project of "decentering the Logos from Western culture." This project aimed to eliminate or *marginalize* Jesus the Logos in order to create a thoroughly secular society. It turns out that postmodernism also entails the elimination of the Greek concept of *logos,* which, as I have explained at length elsewhere and have taught widely, does not mean "rationality," (*ratio* in Latin) but "language" (*verbum* in Latin).

Twenty-some years after the 1974 walkout from Concordia Lutheran Seminary St. Louis, the foundational heresy erupted again at the same LCMS seminary. After being taught for years by a St. Louis professor, the foundational heresy was published for all to see in a confused and confusing book with the duplicitous title, *What Does This Mean? Principles of Biblical Interpretation in the Post-modern World.* The LCMS's Concordia Publishing House published the first edition in 1997 and a second, revised edition in 2001. The book is promoted to this day as "a basic hermeneutics textbook for Christians, especially those of the Lutheran tradition [which] discusses textual criticism, semantics, pragmatics, and [the] application of biblical texts to postmodern contexts [covering] the areas of language, thought, reality, and more."

As reported in the *Concordia Theological Quarterly* (1998), one of my alma maters, our Lutheran seminary in Fort Wayne held a symposium on this "basic hermeneutics textbook for Christians, especially those of the Lutheran tradition." It appears that, in spite of the Fort Wayne faculty's Lutheran sensibility that something unsettling was going on, the contributors to the print version of their symposium spoke in a gentle pro and con way about the book, commending it as a brave new book on hermeneutics from St. Louis, with some contributors adopted the book's semiotic view of language, while giving little attention, if any, either to the book's subtitle or its assertion that teachers and students of Bible interpretation should join in fellowship with postmodernism.

To go by the CTQ journal, Fort Wayne *completely missed the foundational heresy that informs this new "Lutheran" hermeneutic.* Apparently, some contributors were quite comfortable with the book's semiotic view of the biblical text.

Now, even if a commentator has a semiotic philosophy

of language, the "signifier" (I am writing foolishly, in imitation of 2 Corinthians 11) *postmodern* in the book's subtitle should tip him off to what dreadful, anti-logos, pseudo-hermeneutic things were being endorsed in that book and taught in our St. Louis seminary.

This book, its subtitle, and its confused and confusing message were an announcement that our St. Louis seminary had chosen to continue teaching and promoting biblical interpretation done on the basis of the foundational heresy. This postmodern-based "biblical hermeneutic" was apparently accepted at both of our LCMS seminaries, to a greater or lesser degree. Lamentably, it wasn't, and still has not been rejected and condemned as the Scriptures and our Formula require.

A few years ago, I wrote about the postmodern heresy taught in the LCMS textbook *What Does This Mean? Principles of Biblical Interpretation in the Post-modern World* in my essay, "Nisi Per Verbum: A Disputation Concerning Postmodernism and the Pastoral Ministry," published in *Logia* (Reformation 2018).

Let us reason together. As I wrote in the second chapter of *Implosion*, there are two mutually exclusive philosophies of language. The italicized bold labels for these two competing philosophies are from Phillip Cary's book, *Outward Signs: The Powerlessness of External Things in Augustine's Thought* (Cary refers to them as two *views* of biblical language, whereas I speak of them as two philosophies in connection with Colossians 2:8) but the included elaborations are mine.

1. ***External Efficacious Means of Grace***. This is the recognition that the biblical text is itself meaningful and effective. We could say of the text what we say of the sacrament of Holy Communion: There is a real presence here. God is present, speaking in, with, and under the texts

of the Holy Scriptures. The infallible and efficacious words of the biblical text are the means by which God Himself does His work among us. Cary notes that this view was held by Aquinas and Luther.

2. *Expressionist Semiotics*. This is the view that the biblical text is nothing but signs to be decoded, and that what really counts is what is going on in each individual's soul or mind. So, the *semeia* or signs are incidental and serve only as opportunities for us to express our individual inner convictions. This *Neoplatonist* view, Cary explains, was held by Augustine and Calvin. (Cary is the expert; I'm not, but I teach that Augustine was a recovering Neo-Platonist, based on his commentaries and sermons on the Psalms, for example.)

The External Efficacious Means of Grace philosophy is the biblical and Lutheran philosophy. It is the philosophy of language maintained in the Lutheran Confessions, such as the Formula. It is the view of the language of Scripture held by every confessional thinker from Luther onward, Johann Gerhard, for example. The Expressionist Semiotics philosophy is the one espoused, for example, in *What Does This Mean? Principles of Biblical Interpretation in the Post-modern World,* and in the CTQ symposium article "A Valuable Service in Addressing Hermeneutical Issues of the 1990s." None of the published articles make anything of the author's affinity for postmodernism and its methodological incredulity toward all sacrosanct or authoritative texts.

Have our LCMS seminary professors read Derrida? In 1994, three years before the first edition of *What Does This Mean? Principles of Biblical Interpretation in the Post-modern World* was published, there was a roundtable discussion in America in which Jaques Derrida gave his view of the Bible according to his postmodern philosophy of language. Notice how he sees the canonical and authoritative text of the Hebrew Bible as nothing but a springboard to infinite deconstruction in the hands of any interpreter, including (as he mentions in passing), Karl Marx. Here is Derrida in his own words.

> First, I have no stable position on the texts you mentioned, the prophets and the Bible. For me, this is an open field, and I can receive the most necessary provocations from these texts as well as, at the same time, from Plato and others.
>
> In *Spectres of Marx* I try to reconstitute the link between Marx and some prophets through Shakespeare. This does not mean that I am simply a religious person or that I am simply a believer. For me, there is no such thing as "religion." Within what one calls religions—Judaism, Christianity, Islam, or other religions—there are again tensions, heterogeneity, disruptive volcanoes, sometimes texts, especially those of the prophets, which cannot be reduced to an institution, to a corpus, to a system.
>
> *I want to keep the right to read these texts in a way that has to be constantly reinvented. It is something which can be totally new at every moment.* Then I would distinguish between religion and faith. If by religion you mean a set of beliefs, dogmas, or institutions—the church, for example, then I would say that religion not only can but should be deconstructed, sometimes in the name of faith.

As we read in this exceptionally clear explanation (clear, that is, for a postmodernist), the hollow and deceptive (and never–to–be–challenged) philosophy of language taught by postmodernism is this: "Language is utterly without (divine or even human) authority because it is meaningless, meaningless.

**This is the foundational heresy:**

**"I want to keep the right to read these texts in a way that has to be constantly reinvented. It is something which can be totally new at every moment."**

**The enthymeme, or unspoken proposition that follows is, "Therefore, no one gets to tell me that I'm wrong!"**

This pervasiveness in the LCMS of this philosophy of language, this postmodern defiance of authoritative texts, this ultimate deployment of magisterial reason (or magisterial irrationality) over and against the Scriptures and our Lutheran Confessions, is the final concern to which we now turn.

**Be ye doers of the Confessions and not hearers only, deceiving yourselves.**

The foundational heresy of Seminex is very much with us today in the LCMS. I submit to you that the heresy of Seminex has become the philosophical foundation for LCMS institutions such as our Concordia universities, and for our synod's administrators, as we see in their manhandling of faithful Lutheran pastors and professors in the United States, and missionaries in our world mission, contrary to the sacrosanct texts of Scripture and our Lutheran Confessions.

It is important to understand that "Lutheran Church-Missouri Synod" (LCMS) is a compound entity. If we fail to recognize the difference between the Lutheran Church on the one hand and the Missouri Synod on the other hand, we will keep falling into what Martin Luther called "the fallacy of composition and division," and utterly fail to grasp the point. (We Lutheran pastors who studied and preached on Genesis 3 for the First Sunday in Lent read this term when studying Luther's commentary on Genesis 3.) The fallacy of composition happens when we get careless and sloppy with the divine gift of language (*logos* in Greek, from *lego,* gathering together) and mistake a part of something for the whole thing, or vice versa.

There are two parts to the LCMS. First, there is "The Lutheran Church" (LC). This is the Lutheran Church per se, the authentically biblical and "pure Lutheran" church of the Formula of Concord. As the Lutheran confessors and authors declared in the Formula's Brief Summary, Rule, and Norm,

> God's Word alone should be and remain the only standard of doctrine to which the writings of no man should be regarded as equal. Everything should be subjected to God's Word... As we lay down God's Word—the eternal truth—as the foundation, we also introduce and quote these writings [the universal creeds, and the earlier confessions of the Lutheran church written during the lifetime of "the blessed Luther," as a witness of the truth and as the unanimously received, correct understanding of our predecessors who have steadfastly held to the pure doctrine.

When Jesus assures us that Heaven and earth will pass away, but His Word will not pass away (Matthew 25:35), He is not talking about the Missouri Synod but about the Lutheran Church.

The other division of the composite LC-MS is the Missouri Synod (MS). The MS includes synodical officials, district presidents, committees, and bylaws. When our Lord promises that the gates of Hades will not stand against His church (Matthew 16:18), He is not saying anything about boards, policies, organizational structure, institutional presidents, and so on.

However, the expectation when the LC-MS was organized was that the MS component of the composite LCMS would gravitate toward and be motivated by the LC. In other words, *the hyphen was put in place so that we would not fall into the fallacy of equating the Lutheran Church with the Missouri Synod*, a fallacy and a conflation that no one reading and agreeing with the Scriptures and our Confessions, such as the Formula, would ever fall into.

Notwithstanding, there is mounting empirical evidence that the LC-MS composition has drifted dramatically over the past fifty years: the MS has moved farther away from the LC. This could be graphed like this: LC——————MS. At the same time, the MS has managed to exercise more and more deleterious influence over the LC and faithful Lutheran pastors, missionaries, and parishioners, so that our church body has become in practice the LC<MS. The problem, to use a political analogy, is that the LCMS has been developing its own administrative state, its own swamp, not in Washington, D.C. but in St. Louis.

At this point, someone is likely to object that I am being disloyal to my Lutheran church, but that is far from the truth. As I have explained, the Missouri Synod of today is at a distance from the Lutheran Church of the Formula, even while it presumes to lord it over faithful members of the Lutheran Church.

It is also possible that readers may think I am contributing to the demise of the Lutheran Church by rejecting and condemning false doctrine as I do. My response is to point you to the LC, the Lutheran Church of the Formula and the Church of the Christ and His Scriptures. As a fellow Lutheran pastor-professor taught me to say in meetings with synodical inquisitors, "It is of little importance to me if I am evaluated by you or by any human court... The One who evaluates me is the Lord" (1 Corinthians 4:3-4).

The task for our LCMS institutions, such as the Concordia universities, given Concordia University Wisconsin's recent adulterous and very public affair with Woke Marxism, is to repent and to reestablish themselves as Lutheran on the basis of the Formula. If they are not Lutheran—and we are still waiting to see if they have the will and indeed the academic wherewithal and integrity to reform themselves in line with the teaching methodology and curricular content of the Formula of Concord *with which they were originally christened*, then we have another LCMS walkout to analyze. The Formula addresses itself to "the churches and schools" of *the* Lutheran Church.

Concordia University Wisconsin followed the foundational heresy, the Derridean hermeneutic, for the decade that I taught there, but just before and during the first engagements of their war on academic freedom beginning in 2022, they significantly increased their (conscious or unconscious) commitment to Derrida and the foundational heresy: ***I want to keep the right to read these texts in a way that has to be constantly reinvented.***

For example, they rewrote bylaws in their postings for the requirements of the next university president. See *Implosion*, Appendixes B and H. In the months after banishing me from campus, the administration altered the Faculty Handbook, inserting notices that the Handbook policies were subject to change by the administration and regents at any time without notification. Instead of correcting Woke Marxist programs such as their Black Student Union and their Woke

Marxist bias-reporting system, they altered the names but continued the programs, as reported in *The Federalist*.

It is not only bylaws and names of programs that the university changed, in keeping with their postmodern heresy. They are also committed to their "right to read *Bible* texts in a way that has to be constantly reinvented." For example, consider 1 Timothy 2:12, where Saint Paul writes this apostolic mandate to the entire Christian Church: "I do not allow a woman to teach or to have authority over a man; instead, she is to remain quiet." The university is right now exercising its "right" to interpret Scripture as it sees fit by having a woman provost who exercises teaching authority over all faculty members, including the pastors of the Theology Department. This "flagship university of the Concordia University System" is not the only Concordia to exercise this right to reinterpret Scripture as it sees fit. To state the obvious: this right of infinite interpretation is not derived from the Scriptures or the Lutheran Confessions; on the contrary, it comes from the foundational heresy.

By the way, in regard to the Concordia universities, some of our pastors and others have been saying that since there are "good theologians" at this Concordia and that Concordia, therefore the Concordia universities are Lutheran. This is another instance of Luther's fallacy of composition and division. The presence of some faithful pastors and professors on a faculty (which is only one part or division of the university) does not make the university Lutheran. If that were the case, Hillsdale College would be a Lutheran college and Marquette University would be a Lutheran university because they both have solid, confessional Lutheran professors on faculty. Claiming that a university is Lutheran because there are "good people" (which a synonym for "nice people") this rationalizing does not cut it as far as Luther is concerned.

> I am much afraid that the universities will prove to be the great gates of hell, unless they diligently labor in explaining the Holy Scriptures, and engraving them in the hearts of youth. *I advise no one to place his child where the Scriptures do not reign paramount.* Every institution in which men are not *unceasingly occupied with the Word of God* must become corrupt (italics added).

It is an all or nothing proposition. If and only if the universities are governed, in curriculum and in teaching, by the Word of God, are they Lutheran. Again, see The Formula of Concord, Epitome and Solid Declaration, for (a) what the Lutheran churches and schools must teach, with (b) the methodology they must follow: the method of "believing, teaching, and confessing what is true biblical doctrine" *while at the same time* "rejecting and condemning false doctrine." This is the Lutheran formula, straight from the Formula. The Formula is the necessary response to Marquart's call for an authoritative standard or norm in the middle of the continuing crisis created by adherence, consciously or unconsciously, to the foundational heresy:

> The aim is simply to highlight what has always been considered basic and decisive among confessing Lutherans, in order to have in hand a *frame of reference* within which to make sense of our present debates (Kurt Marquart, *Explosion*).

But what is the Missouri Synod's, the MS's, stance toward the frame of reference, the Formula, and how does the MS treat the many faithful pastors, professors, missionaries, and laypeople who expect the LCMS to abide, as they do, by this confessional summary, rule, standard, and norm?

Let's get down to brass tacks. The MS of the LCMS is attacking, dismissing, and shunning steadfast Lutherans (a) on the basis of its own bylaws which, in the day-to-day interactions of synodical officials with Lutheran pastors and parishioners, replace the authoritative texts of the Scriptures and the Formula, (b) while exercising its "right to read these texts in a way that has to be constantly reinvented" (Derrida).

For example, consider this bylaw and the way it is currently being used by the MS.

> 3.8.3.1 The Board for International Mission is charged with developing and determining policies in support of mission and ministry in foreign countries for the Office of International Mission (Bylaw 1.2.1 [n])... liaison with the colleges, universities, and seminaries of the Synod... international schools ...
>
> Upon the recommendation of the Office of International Mission, the board shall serve as the only sending agency through which workers and funds are sent to the foreign mission areas of the Synod, including the calling, appointing, assigning, withdrawing, and releasing of missionaries (ministers of religion–ordained and ministers of religion–commissioned) and other workers for the ministries in foreign areas.

This bylaw is not based on the authority of Scripture and the Confessions, despite the preamble of qualifications in The 2019 Handbook, where bylaws begin on page 20. No doubt the synodical reply from those in the various mission boards will be, "Our authority to act as the only agency to allocate funding, to call or release missionaries, and so on, comes from the synod in convention." But this is an especially offensive *ad populam* fallacy. Divine calls are not based on democratic voting but on the Word of God as it is written and on our Confessions because they are, in turn, under the sole authority of the written Word.

This damnable bylaw (the Latin word in the Formula's mandate to *condemn* false doctrine is *damnamus*) is currently being used by synod officials to invalidate the divine call of the director of our Lutheran School of Theology in Kenya. In addition, synodical members of various mission boards and the Concordia University System have been communicating with the pastors of parishes that faithfully support the Lutheran School of Theology, urging them to see to it that their congregations and their parishioners stop supporting the School and stop inviting our director to preach in LCMS congregations.

The MS's conduct in "developing and determining policies in support of mission and ministry in foreign countries" has caused great harm to called missionaries and indeed to mission work worldwide. In Africa, where it is estimated that almost half of the souls on the continent speak French, MS oversight has degraded the number of French-speaking Lutheran missionaries from 12 to one in the last decade or so. The one remaining missionary, in great demand in *many* African countries as a powerful preacher and the primary teacher of Lutheran doctrine, is the director of the congregation-funded and accredited Lutheran School of Theology. When an African academic I know heard this thing, he remarked on the racial prejudice of the MS for opposing the one theological school he knows about that plans to hand over its curriculum and facilities to faithful African Lutherans in fulfillment of its mission to "form African Lutherans to teach the faith."

On another mission front, as reported in *Christian News*, "The LCMS recently caused a major division within a partner church in Sri Lanka." LCMS overreach and incompetence have obliged faithful missionaries and pastors to prepare a proposal for the next synodical convention to establish a new district for world missionaries because there is no due process for missionaries in the LCMS. Whereas in Seminex 1.0 those in the wrong staged a walkout, in Seminex 2.0 those in the wrong are staging a sit-in within the boards and offices of the LCMS—to the great harm of the Lord's work and the Lord's called workers. MS officials believe they have the right to interpret things as they want and will, according to their endless interpretations of the biblical text. I imagine none of them has read Derrida; nonetheless, they have bought into the foundational heresy of postmodernism. Perhaps they learned this from reading *What Does This Mean? Principles of Biblical Interpretation in the Post-modern World.* I have been told by faithful pastors in the field that devotees of that book have for years been practicing postmodernism in Spanish mission venues.

In the States, the MS's affinity for asserting its "right to read these texts in a way that has to be constantly reinvented" (Derrida) came to light nationally because of the CUW / LCMS / CUS's assault on academic freedom. For the footnotes on this scandal, please see Appendixes I-N in *Implosion*. Here is an insight into how LCMS district presidents have both substituted synodical bylaws for the authoritative texts of the Bible and our Confessions, while at the same time maintaining their "right to read these texts in a way that has to be constantly reinvented."

In their hurry to find a way to punish me further for calling out the false doctrine of Woke Marxism at Concordia University Wisconsin after their blatant failure to provide due process (just like the MS's conduct against our missionaries) the administration decided to "invent something new" by using a synodically approved document titled "2020 Model Operating Manual, Faculty and Administration Complaints and Appeal of Termination: Colleges and Universities." Although that text was for *appealing* terminations, not for imposing terminations after denying due process, a synod official okayed its novel use for seeking termination. Although the administration and regents had failed to follow the procedure as stated in the Operating Manual, the synod-selected committee chairman, a lawyer, went ahead with the illegitimate procedure. Although the Manual specified that no one could serve on the committee if there was even the appearance of bias, a very recently retired district president who had misrepresented my entire situation in an email to the entire Michigan District would not recuse himself, nor would the chairman eliminate him from the committee, and on and on.

When it came to the testimony of witnesses, I asked another district president, the only witness willing to speak against me, in front of the chairman and his committee, "Do you acknowledge the authority of Scripture and the Confessions, particularly Luther's explanation of the Eighth Commandment and its concluding paragraphs about what is at issue in this proceeding?" His response was, "I have authority over you according to the bylaws." I repeated my question. He gave the same response but added, "And according to the bylaws, I have handed you over to the university to do what they need to do. After that, I will take care of you myself." I asked a third time if he acknowledged the authority of Scripture and Luther's Large Catechism on the matter at hand. At that point, the chairman declared in a lawyerly fashion, "Asked and answered; move on."

The collars of the synodical officials on mission boards, serving as district presidents, conniving new, inventive ways of interpreting synodical texts against called pastors, and so on, wear the white collars of men of God whose throats should be speaking the pure Word of God; but their voices are the voice of Derrida: "I want the right to read these texts in a way that has to be constantly reinvented." And no one gets to tell them that they are wrong, we are told again and again. However, as we are instructed by the Formula,

> It is not only necessary that the pure, wholesome doctrine be rightly presented ... but it is also necessary that the opponents who teach otherwise be reproved ... No one should be misled in this matter by the reputation of any person.

## Conclusion

As I wrote at the beginning of this essay, I am especially concerned with what shows up in the Greek use of *hairesis* as a verb in the middle voice, where the user of the heresy is simultaneously (a) promulgating the heresy and (b) working under its influence, whether consciously or unconsciously. As I have shown in this philosophical study of modernism and postmodernism, the foundational heresy of Seminex was what we now call *postmodernism*.

By quoting Derrida's 1994 comments regarding his interpretation of the Bible, I demonstrated that postmodernism is utterly opposed to the authoritative Word of God. Postmodernism opposes the Word of Christ by willfully asserting, **"I want to keep the right to read these texts in a way that has to be constantly reinvented. It is something which can be totally new at every moment."**

Consciously or unconsciously, the following persons and entities of the LCMS based or are basing their interpretation of the Bible and lesser authoritative texts on the foundational heresy of postmodernism:

- First, the Seminex professors of the 1970s from the LCMS seminary in St. Louis.

- Secondly, the author of the textbook *What Does This Mean?: Principles of Biblical Interpretation in the Post-Modern World*, published initially in 1997 and then in a revised edition in 2001 by the LCMS's Concordia Publishing House. The author was a professor at the seminary in St. Louis.

- Notably, there was little, if any, reaction against the LCMS text *What Does This Mean?* from the faculty of our other LCMS seminary at Concordia Theological Seminary in Fort Wayne in 1998.

- Thirdly, there is the evidence of Concordia University Wisconsin, "the flagship university of the LCMS's Concordia University System," copiously documented by external reporting from *The Federalist*, by texts from national authorities, and by the university's willingness to invent and rewrite procedural and institutional governance texts; as well as its flagrant reinterpreting of biblical texts such as 1 Timothy 2:12.

- Fourthly, there is mounting evidence of the synodical administrators and district presidents' manifest commitment to the foundational heresy of postmodernism in their attacks on faithful pastors in North America and in overseas mission fields, showing in words and actions that they are in fellowship with postmodernism: "***I want to keep the right to read these texts in a way that has to be constantly reinvented. It is something which can be totally new at every moment.***"